DOOR TO A NOISY ROOM

DOOR TO A
NOISY ROOM

Peter Waldor

Alice James Books
Farmington, Maine

10 9 8 7 6 5 4 3 2 1

Alice James Books are published by Alice James Poetry Cooperative, Inc., an affiliate of the University of Maine at Farmington.

ALICE JAMES BOOKS
238 MAIN STREET
FARMINGTON, ME 04938

www.alicejamesbooks.org

LIBRARY OF CONGRESS CATALOGING-IN-PUBLICATION DATA
Waldor, Peter, 1963–
Door to a noisy room / Peter Waldor
   p.   cm.
ISBN-13: 978–1–882295–66–1
ISBN-10: 1–882295–66–8
I. Title.
PS3623.A3569.D66 2008
811'.6—dc22   2007025121

Alice James Books gratefully acknowledges support from the University of Maine at Farmington and the National Endowment for the Arts. ❦

Cover Art: Two Dancers, late Roman mosaic, Vestibule of the Scala del Bramante. Location : Museo Pio Clementino. Photo Credit : Scala / Art Resource, NY.

for Jody, Jacob, Nathaniel & Gabriel

CONTENTS

I

II

ACKNOWLEDGMENTS

Many thanks to the following journals where these poems
(sometimes in earlier versions) first appeared:

2River: "Dancer"

420: "'Heart and Soul' On the Piano"

American Poetry Review: "Straits," "Moon," "Perfect Islamic Bliss,"
   "Moloch and Jesus," "Insurance Man," "A New Religion,"
   "Blue Bells"

Iowa Review: "Pear of My Nose . . . ," "Future," "Temporary
   Disfigurement," "On The Buttocks," "Insurance"

Margie: "Frigidaire," "Goodbye Manny Seepe"

Mudlark: "A Man Touches A Woman's Cream Jar,"
   "Honeymoon," "South Orange Winter," "Milk Humility"

Ploughshares: "The Passing Ark," "The Hive Quiet For Now,"
   "Spine"

Potomac Review: "Ribs"

Sugar Mule: "Lips," "A Map," "Nose"

Tikkun: "Sadder Than Abraham"

West Branch: "Touch," "Like Me"

Lips

My love, our lips
are four knives
asleep in the drawer.

Last four left.
The rest out for
the usual butchery.

The craftsmen—
the woodworker,
silversmith,

gone for good;
even the glassblower
who puffed the knob

that has gone
unheld all evening
is gone.

Spine

The spine is a seahorse
swimming in the body.
The spine is inside hair gone stiff.
The spine leaks ideas
the way cardboard leaks water.
Submerged saw.
Feller of forests.
Felled by forests.
The spine is innocent.
The body guilty.
Just as skin bleeds,
the spine bleeds.
Just as hair grows after death,
so does the spine.
Weld of top to bottom.
The spine's speech is half
good clock, half slipping gears.
The spine is most like the nose.
In fact we once breathed through the spine,
though now, as you know, we just eat and sleep.

Temporary Disfigurement

Bless temporary disfigurement
for it begins and ends.
A man combs the hills
to collect the severed parts.
He sews so awkwardly it seems there cannot
be brilliance and perfection
but they are there in the very awkwardness,
and after all it is not centuries but afternoons
and the man is whole again,
torn and repaired.
He stares at his arms
before he forgets them,
before he forgets the surgeon,
and he is ready for love after the terrible solitude,
and for solitude, of course.

Brothel Guide

Brother is one letter
from brothel.
A brother
told me Freud
loved to wander
in the red light district.
Red, shade
of accident
and quietness.
I am so happy
I run,
hat in hand.
If I kill
or am killed,
my brother
and the father
of the mind
are the real killers.
Arrest them.

Like Me

Down the hall
a crone folds towels
and here, a fresh
towel, plastic tulip.
The stairs have turned
so many times
there is no city below.
Are others like me:
ruthless and brilliant
before love, and afterwards,
a lamb?

Seriously

Who knows whether
she is a great whore
or just serious.
I know just one
of her four languages.
Other than love, nothing
can put me to sleep.

Slowness Is All of Love

Truth is I don't remember
whether it was Poem II
with the *bough of fruit*
falling from the sun
or Poem XIV with *what spring*
does to cherry trees
that my darling whispered.
And I don't remember her name
which was not her name.

A Man Touches a Woman's Cream Jar

A split sea,
hawthorn hedge,
elevator,
honor guard,
dusky hallway
and the man is before
the glass shelves
and the jar,
the trade of Crete
or Jamaica;
for all great jars
come from islands;
for a jar is an island.
It is enough to touch
the secret,
forefinger and third
against the wall.
Inside, a thimbleful
of cream,
enough for a lifetime,
for a daughter to try,
but I digress,
for the man removed
his fingers
and has no theory.
No one knows of his journey.
Not even the woman
will notice her jar
has moved an inch
among the others,
the brushes,
the pastes.

On the Buttocks

Constantine P. Cavafy
is naked. Nice ass!
He walks around the block
and waves like the Pope.
The buttocks are a little
like breasts,
a little like heads.
Two better than one.
Neighbors
scatter rose petals
in our hero's path.
The buttocks are closets
full of heirlooms.
There is a dark slash
between them,
like a space between pages.
Ottomans.
Moons.
Excuses
for dainty cloth.
All our lives we hear
there is one moon
and everywhere
we see two.
Now and then
someone from the crowd
dashes for a touch,
for luck,
to tell grandchildren,
and not to wash.

Pear of My Nose . . .

A man who lingers
in the market if
a good song is on.
A man who picks
bruised fruit, carefully
as the rest of us choose
the beauties, knowing no one
would take them.
He pares the bruises
away in the kitchen
and eats them before
he brings the bowl for me.

Touch

Light that matters most
is light good for nothing.
And though we call the worst
of this sick world *shit,*
the lovers, who believe
they are the first lovers,
sigh and embrace and smile.
They touch each other
about their assholes.
They are not struck dead.

Straits

One great culture is not
destroying another today.
A boy straightens
the black hair of another boy,
a mother's work.
Old comb in his fist.
A great patience
between brothers,
through with a swim
in the wakes of cargo ships
and explorers.

Perfect Islamic Bliss

Four daisies
by the mosque window
when I look up
from prayer,
and blowing
from town
the smoke
of a guitar.
Simple daisies.
Simple.
The window
could be a painting.
The distant player
just practicing.

A New Religion

A man ties a cord
around his old coat.

Hostile country,
he camps with no fire or water.

Fresh blood of dusk
darkens to old blood, then black.

In his dream, a white flower
and sparrows, each beak on a petal.

Kingdoms away, in a satchel,
a manuscript, the man's story,

though no dream with flower and birds.
No final dream.

Moon

A crescent is nearly nothing,
like the joke
where a poor man
prays "Lord, I am nothing"
and one rebbe says to the other rebbe
"Look who's being a nothing!"

Moloch and Jesus

I am sure it is Moloch and Jesus in the skiff!
Each wave, a curtain that hides
the craft in an empty sea.
A bare-chested rower
and two men, backs to us, in robes.
Look at us in the surf!
Sandals on and cloaks hitched,
a letter from the governor and flowers.

Sadder Than Abraham

Sadder than Abraham
with his spattered frock.
Sadder than Isaac,
skidding down
the mountain alone,
seeing the trees
as if for the first time.
Sadder than the ram,
its head in the dust.
Sadder than this troupe
is the thicket
which held the ram.
Even with a scroll
of crimes it weeps
for the horns
in its brambles,
the blood it drew.
The thicket that listened
to the yelp and silence,
yelp and silence,
like a door to a noisy room
opening and closing.

The Enemy's Music

No desert wind and the olive
won't bloom; if it blows
too soon the wheat will scorch.

The village is at the altar,
making sacrifice.
My daughter left flowers.

Damascus radio
sets the sun in the sea.
How lovely, the enemy's music.

Passing Ark

Tonight I won't dance
by the ark.
If they pound
on my door—
the dancers
with loose shirts,
whooping
over the storm—
I will snuff the light
and hold Michal.
Let the comet pass.
Michal's bread is finished—
we leave it.

Uriah the Hittite

A sage
called Uriah,
a terrible enemy
of Israel.

I, the simpleton,
knew him only
as loyal
soldier, husband.

Lord, if you take
my house away,
don't wait
for my children.

Masters

Rain on leaves.
Steps on staircases.
Stop.
The masters failed
to pass through
the needles
with their sheaves
of poems.

Dancer

I could never restrain myself
enough to be a dancer,
never let my fingers
snow on the back.
I could never adore the master.
When a partner was covered
with sores, I vomited.
When I have nothing to do
I do nothing.

Ebed Melech, the Ethiopian Eunuch

Three young men
study the Bible
in the Roman
Gourmet Pizzeria.
The famous opium quote
comes to mind,
but as a young man,
my Bible was just
as dog-eared.
I want to ask about
their favorite part.
I could tell how
Ebed Melech threw rags
to Jeremiah in the pit,
who wedged them
under his waterlogged
arms when Ebed pulled
him up with a rope.
The young men may
never know the name
of the greatest
hero of all time.

Blue Bells

The terrible thing
about leaving paradise—
the thought I could

be entering paradise.
No tollgates, no fences.
Blue bells everywhere.

As petals leave
the bud, the bud
is surprised, focusing

for so long,
then looking away
at the exact

wrong moment.
A boy is not even
a young man when

he forgets the embrace
of his father.
I am told my father

wore a blue robe
when he held me
in the dark.

Future

Poets will quit
before all talk vanishes.
The cabins will be built.

The fireplaces.
I'll be long gone,
ripped apart. I hope

I get a hand on my heart,
so I can tear it out
and hold it like a sweet roll,

toss it to an enemy.
A river better jump
its bank for my head.

Nose

Why weren't we Polish
noblemen like normal people?
My father away at cavalry;
my mother on a divan chatting
with the Cracow Count,
her nose one stroke
from the Japanese watercolor
on the wall at her back.
It is the indefatigable Count
who offers the comparison
and my mother pretends
she does not hear, tapping
a mahogany arm, a fist
of blond hair in a bun.

Loved to Play Dead

As a child he loved
to play dead
and he never outgrew it,
so there he was
at fifty, grabbing
his chest, writhing
and collapsing.
He did it for laughs,
but once someone
had a heart attack.
He loved to roll
down steps in front
of a crowd.
I was his shill.
I lifted him over
my shoulder and hobbled
a few steps before
I too collapsed,
and you know what.

Insurance

for Jerry Waldor

My father and I,
salesmen ourselves,
said no to a man
selling roses.
The road, a whip
laid on the land.
Both quiet
after declining.
My father drives,
I give directions.

The Guilt of Elevators

I weep for the power
used in elevators
to lift just me.
Store it up,
and churches
could be built.
The guilt
of elevators is worse
than the guilt of cars.
The guilt of elevators
is hidden.
We never even
hum the hum
of the elevator.
The elevator slides
in its channel.
Faint rattler.
Melting pot.
Don't forget
the rare plummet
despite the missing
number.
Don't argue land
or counterweights.
Remember when
they put mirrors
in the corners?
I weep for the power,
but I pray
no one comes aboard,
no one sees me.

South Orange Winter

The trees honest now.
I hope for fog, cloud
with broken strings.
A policeman on a stoop
cracks pistachios
before he storms the house.
Thin jacket unzipped.
The suspect asleep.

Nisus and Euryalus

Behind enemy lines
the henchmen go

sleeper to sleeper
slitting throats until

Nisus is so excited
he shouts.

Once, in a matter of life
and death, when quietness

was also a matter
of life and death,

I laughed. Virgil
tells us a glint

from stolen armor
gave the henchmen away;

why he never mentions
the shout, we don't know.

Two Sessions in Trenton

White men are lovely
but I was sad
at the new police
captains' training session.

Not one caterpillar
among them,
not one perfume
among the colognes.

And in the next room,
women,
mostly snowflakes
of other colors,

studied to help
death row prisoners.
Perhaps
Reverend Moon

will do a group wedding
for the captains and volunteers?
How marvelous, the moving
arch of the caterpillar!

Think how long
it took to copy it,
and that only
in stationary form.

Goodbye Manny Seepe

Parking meter
to parking meter,
collector of the smallest tax,
you were most innocent,
you hummingbird,
you sprite who capered.
White socks.
Some streams
find no others,
Manuel:
bird, laugher,
tennis player,
never anyone's teacher,
goodbye.

Got Milk? Billboard

The turnpike packed
but all the cars whizz
over the limit

like neurons up
and down the shaking
leg of a mosquito

that can barely hold
a belly of fresh
blood as it lifts off.

Should I single out
a man who bribed
a county clerk

for his billboard spot,
and not mention
the other thieves?

The man happens
to be a friend
and I hate to see

a friend make
money
so easily.

Insurance Man

All my life I dreamed
of being a shepherd,
not an insurance man.
A shepherd said,
The Lord is my shepherd.
Shepherds always
want a shepherd.
Even the Lord asks.

Night Sale

Gold initials
nearly
rubbed out.
The briefcase
prongs snap
like snare drums.
A smell of old
cologne curls
like a genie.
An overripe
voice addresses
death, quietly,
a ring
on the pinkie
like one book
at the end
of a shelf.
Lucky night—
on the last
onion skin,
a signature,
wet and blue.

Handshake

Very small is very beautiful
where the vein shakes
hands with the artery;
shake of strangers
who sense they want
to be friends.
Once, my father surprised
me by shaking my hand.
Once, he spilled a basket
of peaches into a stream.

Intravenous Pole

Who left
the IV pole
on the hospital
roof for our
pleasure?
Dare I call it cross-shaped?
The dull arm does cross
the stainless pole.
Threads inside
gummed up,
like so many
valleys full
of silt.
Long gone,
the old bags.
Long gone,
what splashed.
Dare I call it
staff-shaped?
It gleams.
Dare I dream
someone
threw it
through
a window
onto the roof
below?
Too much.
Some last
words were
Too much.
Not enough.

Ribs

Once I saw a doctor break a man's ribs,
a dead man, to see why he died.
Plowed fields under snow.
I hear the rasp of blade in earth,
more a whisper, more a shirt
stripped off a chest. Ribs,
the good doctor was only passing
through on her way to a kidney
and a stalled river; just a drifter passing through.
I admire drifters.

IV

Honeymoon

High in the ruins,
reaching for my hand,
my love fell backwards.
There was only grass
where paving stones once
would have broken her.
I led her slowly down
to port where everyone
was gone, just an octopus
left strung on a pole.
At the end of the day,
one unclaimed monster
for our pleasure.

Gold Rings

Today's diamonds were sweat
and tears of joy, much rarer
than sweat and those other tears.

My love and I, in the sun,
were blessed by a beautiful
young woman, a sage.

Compared to me, my love
cries more easily
and is more impervious to pain.

She who lifts things
from fires and weeps
at bird flight.

Honeymoon Guitars

Tonight, guitars
while a gale rattles
the house.

Explorers
blown off course—
so no epics,

just us
on a mountain
of song,

wind so strong
the stench
from the slaughterhouse

down the way is gone.
On its roof,
a pile of horns,

sacrifice to no god,
unless they are
blown away.

A Map

I led my father up a mountain.
On top, we laughed in the spring snow.
I, who look like his mother,
and he who won't look at me.
I gave him a map, which he lost.
Later, in town, we saw a breeze
knock the blossoms
off a cherry tree.

Milk Humility

Halfway up the window,
halfway to heaven,
a pint of milk is balanced
on the cool pane.
The drinker takes
an afternoon to sip.
If slats, frame and glass
are forgotten, there is just
a floating carton.
The hillside beyond
has not blossomed.
The milk has not blossomed.
The drinker has not.

The Hive Quiet for Now

Sons gone,
my parents quiet
in their mountain kitchen.
A last tomato quartered.
A long time ago my mother
ran up the mountain
trailed by yellow jackets
like the train of a dress.
A groundhog
squeezes into the garden.
In the valley a building
goes up in smoke.
They call the smoke a scarf.
They know better.

Frigidaire

My father and brother
knock into the Frigidaire
and the motor stops—
not broken, resting.
The wrestlers don't notice.
The frail man will live,
but the young genius?
Neither grunts.

Carrot, Cabbage, Broccoli, Cucumber, Lettuce, Onion, Squash

My love,
in black,
is pure.
No flowers,
no hashmarks,
but not so pure
she worries.
I fail
in her dreams.
Once I died
of cancer.
Once I fled
in a boat
with a prostitute.
So, she never
lets me from
her sight
and she taught me
seven vegetables.
Her sight, I love,
and vegetables,
naturally.

Yelling About Holiness

In civilization we rush
leaves away

so there is nothing to kick
and remember the Master chasing

one leaf, his students in tow,
yelling about holiness.

I saw a mother, father and son playing,
just heavy shirts, no gloves, no hats,

chasing each other, yelling
"I am king of the world."

No Masters left, just a few scientists
among the remnant of the Jews.

"Heart and Soul" on the Piano

In the grammar school by the quarry;
in the lunch paradise;
in the original gymnasium;
child dancers, both eleven,
dance at their wedding
and laugh at the joke of music.
Under the boy's slacks,
driftwood.
Scholars ask "Is it art?"

Homophobia

Reading to my children
before bed, I skipped
where Ovid tells how Orpheus
forswore women for boys
because boys were like fresh
flowers, and I started again
where the women tore him apart
and his head rolled in the river.

Feet

The feet are the lips of the body.
Deep drinkers.
Printed on one side,
blank on the other.
Locked in wool.
We chant
against their appearing
without veils—
insurrection.
Battering rams,
but sensitive.
Earth hinges.
Prophets in the same town—
they don't talk.
Who knows
whether they
begin or end?
Blue rivers.
Shields.
Pink pontoons.
Ten in all.
From one a skiff shoves off,
a perfumed letter
on the rower's breast.
The brave rower
hides his craft
and slips into port;
gown whistling,
feet, rapid on the paving,
soft applause.

Hands

Not eyes,
but hands,
where souls
hold court.
Gears clear.
Smooth
as old stoops.
First to age.
Most youthful.
Of course
we read them
and won't talk
without them.
They say
thank you,
goodbye.
Hand on hip—
open sesame.
The hand,
a brush—
makes
a brushing
sound when I
try to touch
my love
so lightly
she feels nothing,
but she always
sighs
and says my name.

Warmth

The ones I love
strip shirts,
pants, underwear
and leave them
behind in a pile,
explorers leaving
a campsite.
They have no idea
I lift the old clothes
one after another
to feel the warmth
still in them.
Who will tell me
to put them down?

Recent Titles from Alice James Books

Alice James Books has been publishing exclusively poetry since 1973. One of the few presses in the country that is run collectively, the cooperative selects manuscripts for publication through both regional and national annual competitions. New regional authors become active members of the cooperative, participating in the editorial decisions of the press. The press, which historically has placed an emphasis on publishing women poets, was named for Alice James, sister of William and Henry, whose fine journal and gift for writing went unrecognized within her lifetime.

TYPESET AND DESIGNED BY MIKE BURTON

Printed by Thomson-Shore
on 50% postconsumer recycled paper
processed chlorine-free